FORTNITE 2020

FORTNITE 2020
ISBN: 978-1-78106-703-1

THIS BOOK
BELONGS TO

_____

CONTENTS

What's inside your new Fortnite annual?!

101 THINGS TO DO IN FORTNITE!

Have you ticked off all of these? Pages 10, 28 and 44!

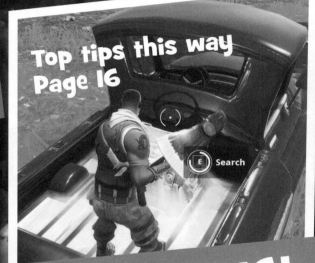

Top tips this way
Page 16

E Search

GET BUILDING!

Page 38

E
SWAP

CAN YOU FLOSS LIKE A BOSS?!

BIG QUIZ!

Put your Fortnite knowledge to the test!

Page 50

+ 100

AMAZING FORTNITE FACTS

Whether you're a seasoned pro or a complete newbie, there's tonnes to learn about your favourite game. Let's start off with a whole bunch of Fortnite facts!

Fortnite was first announced in 2011, but it kept getting PUSHED BACK until it was eventually RELEASED IN 2017! The wait was clearly worth it – just TWO MONTHS after the game was made available it already had ONE MILLION PLAYERS!

A group of STUDENTS from Ohio recently made a bet with their teacher that if they could get 6,700 RETWEETS, their FINAL EXAM would have to be made up exclusively of questions about FORTNITE. The tweet was shared 30,000 times and as a result the exam QUESTIONS WERE REWRITTEN to include Fortnite references!

Although BATTLE ROYALE is the most POPULAR MODE, it DIDN'T EXIST at launch! It wasn't added until late 2017 thanks to the popularity of PLAYERUNKNOWN BATTLEGROUNDS, which was the first game to experience BIG SUCCESS with a Battle Royale mode. Fortnite's Battle Royale mode took just TWO WEEKS to hit 10 MILLION PLAYERS!

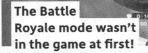

The Battle Royale mode wasn't in the game at first!

The CELEBRATORY DANCE MOVES are a FAVOURITE PART of the game, but they've been known to get the makers in hot water. The company has only narrowly won LAWSUITS claiming that the DANCE MOVES were used WITHOUT PERMISSION from their creators!

The dance moves got Epic in trouble!

On the flip side, FOOTBALL AND RUGBY LEAGUE PLAYERS have been spotted using FORTNITE DANCE MOVES as part of their scoring CELEBRATIONS!

Over 200 million players means no shortage of opponents

The NUMBERS FOR FORTNITE are insane! There are over 200 MILLION PLAYERS, with up to 10 MILLION CONCURRENT PLAYERS. It's no wonder you're never SHORT OF OPPONENTS! It has topped the ITUNES CHART in 13 COUNTRIES with over 82.6 MILLION downloads.

Thanos briefly joined the game!

Don't worry, though, as at least MARVEL isn't worried about POTENTIAL COPYRIGHT INFRINGEMENT. In 2018, it actually PUT THANOS and the INFINITY GAUNTLET into the game to tie in with the release of AVENGERS: INFINITY WAR. The NEW MODE was a HUGE HIT, with some fans asking for it to come back permanently!

The FORTNITE MAP is always CHANGING and, perhaps most hilariously, one BUILDING has been DESTROYED REPEATEDLY. Found in TILTED TOWERS, it was demolished by the METEOR STRIKE in SEASON 3, spent SEASON 4 in RUINS, was REBUILT over SEASON 5, and reopened as a SPORTING GOODS STORE just in time to be destroyed by THE CUBE in SEASON 6. It's currently well on its way to being rebuilt!

Fortnite is based on the UNREAL ENGINE 4 which POWERS HUNDREDS OF GAMES, including CRACKDOWN 3, DAYS GONE, GEARS OF WAR 4, LIFE IS STRANGE, PLAYERUNKNOWN'S BATTLEGROUNDS, AND STREET FIGHTER V!

The SKINS are based on loads of characters. The SKELETON OUTFIT looks like a COBRA KAI member from the 80s movie THE KARATE KID. CODENAME E.L.F. is based on WILL FERRELL'S costume from the ELF movie. RUST LORD is a version of STAR LORD from the GUARDIANS OF THE GALAXY movie!

PART I

101 AMAZING THINGS TO DO IN FORTNITE

There's an unbelievable amount of content in Fortnite, so here's our ultimate list of 101 brilliant things you need to do in the game!

Wall up an enemy!

1 Wall up an enemy so they can't get out, then run off and leave them in their freshly built prison!

2 If you spot a loot crate dropping, use jump pads to propel yourself into the air and land on top of it. Not only is it fun, it will get you to the loot quicker!

3 Find the hidden rooms! From the bunker in the forest to the treasure chest room in the tomato tunnel, locating these extra spaces will give you a real edge.

4 Lure an enemy onto a jump pad, then when they're in the air use them as target practice. Not quite a sitting duck, but still very easy to deal with!

5 Did you know it's possible to jump on a rocket after it's been fired? There's no real value to this and it will probably result in a quick death, but boy is it fun!

Hide in a bush!

6 Use the boogie bomb on your enemies to humiliate them before you punch their ticket to the afterlife!

7 Drink the bush potion (which camouflages you as a bush!), then see how close you can get to another player without them spotting you.

8 Watch TV! If you find a TV in a building, you can switch it on and see what's playing. There are a few different shows – just remember to watch your back too!

9 Shoot the top off a fire hydrant and ride the stream of water high into the air. Just make sure you land somewhere safe, otherwise it will be the last thing you do in the game.

10 Find the soccer field and have a kick about! The location tends to change based on which version you're playing but there's usually one somewhere.

Only use melee weapons

Delay opening your glider

11 See how far you can fall without the glider opening. You can delay it longest by falling above open water!

12 There's a second version of the battle bus hidden on the east side of the map. See if you can find it!

13 See how high you can build before someone comes and tries to follow you, then sneak down and destroy the tower from under them!

14 See how far you get using just melee weapons and no guns! It's tough to make even one kill, but not impossible!

15 Play the game in Creative mode and see what sort of things you can build – maybe try to copy stuff from other games like Minecraft!

16 Don't worry about fighting – land on one side of the map and see if you can run in a straight line to the other without being killed or ambushed!

17 Restrict yourself to one building shape, so for an entire game you should ONLY use ramps, for example. Or roofs if you want to make it extra difficult for yourself!

18 In Squad mode, agree that if one of you dies, you all stop fighting immediately – if one of you goes down, you ALL go down.

19 Join a duo and agree that one of you won't use any guns – the job of the other player is to protect them from being killed for as long as possible!

20 Collect as many resources as possible, then when the storm circle starts shrinking, build a skybridge and try not to touch the ground again for the rest of the game!

21 Make a rule that you HAVE to collect every weapon you see and switch to it, even if it's worth less than the weapon you're using.

Use just one building shape

Only build with one material

22 Here's a challenge: you can only build with the first type of material you collect and nothing else for the rest of the game!

23 See how many players you can kill by using ONLY traps. And pat yourself on the back if it's more than one!

24 Make sure you shoot at EVERY enemy you see. No stealth allowed! Even if you've only got a shotgun and no chance to kill them, you HAVE to fire.

25 Put the letters A-J and the numbers 1-10 in a hat and pick them out before a game. This is the grid reference you have to try to land in when you jump!

26 Immediately use every item you find, even if there's no one else around. Don't carry anything except guns and ammo!

27 Play a round without using ANY med kits or bandages. If you're really hardcore, make sure you don't use any healing items at all!

Land on a specific grid reference

28 Pretend you can't reload weapons and chuck them away as soon as you run out of ammo!

29 When you land near an interesting location, try to protect it as long as the storm eye allows you to. Make sure no one else gets in!

30 Make sure you only ever enter houses by smashing a hole in the wall. Never enter through the door!

31 Run to the very centre of the storm eye every time it changes, and try to survive there. Take care – it will probably be a popular place!

32 Throw grenades as soon as you collect them – pretend they're already primed to explode, chuck them, then run!

33 Never reload your gun automatically – make every shot count and only let the clip reload itself.

34 Only collect loot from houses on the first floor or higher – nothing you find on the ground floor is allowed!

Only collect loot from the first floor

10 QUICK TIPS TO FORTNITE SUCCESS!

Looking to hit the ground running in a game of Fortnite? Follow these quick tips!

I.

FIND LOOT FAST!

You're not going to get far in Fortnite without some weapons! Learn where to find chests, and find one fast! If two of you are landing on the same spot, it's a straight race to get to the weapons first!

2.

KEEP MOVING

Nothing says 'sitting duck' like somebody standing still in the middle of a Fortnite map!

3.

SHIELDS UP!

Once you're armed, get yourself shield potions! Get to at least 50 shields as fast as you can. You'll need it come a big firefight!

10 QUICK TIPS TO FORTNITE SUCCESS!

4.

RESOURCES

Chop down some trees early, and make sure you have the resources to quickly build a ramp or some defences!

HEADPHONES!

Having headphones makes it easier to pick out the small audio clues – someone sneaking around, for instance – that you may not ordinarily get with speakers!

5.

PICK YOUR MOMENT

When you see an enemy, first check whether they've seen you. If they haven't, choose your moment to take them out. Once you fire, they'll very much know you're there!

6.

HIGH!

As the game progresses, you're at a real advantage if you have a higher position! You're tougher to hit, and it's easier to land a shot with more accuracy.

7.

9.

YOU CAN AVOID BUILDING...

...but you stand a much better chance of winning a Battle Royale if you at least master the building basics!

10.

JUMP AROUND!

If you're in a close-quarters firefight, jump! Keep jumping, make yourself harder to hit, and make every shot count!

8.

BALANCE YOUR WEAPONS

Ideally, you want a mix of a sniper rifle, a shotgun, and a faster-fire weapon such as an assault rifle.

0 | 100
+ 100 | 100

THE BUILDING GUIDE

Want to become a master builder? Discover how to put together any kind of structure!

140 HP

EDIT

MATERIAL

Smash items to collect materials

BATTLE BUS LAUNCHING IN 9

MATERIALS

In Fortnite, there are only three building materials:

Wood is easy to collect from trees. If you're in an urban zone, look for pallets and fences. Although it's quick to build using wood, the structures are quite weak and vulnerable to attack.

Stone can be collected from rocks in rural areas, and concrete walls/ buildings in urban areas, which makes it relatively common. It takes a little longer to build using stone, but it's stronger than wood.

Metal is common in urban areas, where it can be collected from vehicles and machinery, but is extremely hard to find in rural areas! Metal is the strongest material you can use to build forts, which is why it's rarer than the other two materials.

BUILDING

The exact way to build depends on which version of the game you're playing, but there are a few common controls. You first need to switch to the building inventory (away from your weapons inventory), then you can use various keys to select, place, rotate and delete the four main parts of a structure. You can also switch the material being used and place a trap if you have one.

Check the controls for your version of the game, as unfortunately we can't list them all here!

Vehicles are good for metal

SMG

Walls

Walls are the simplest of the four main shapes. You can use them to quickly set up defensive structures that hide you on all sides. Just spin around, placing four walls around you, and you'll create a basic enclosure that can even be used as the base for a larger fort.

A standard wall is a 3x3 panel, and you can edit bits of it to create other basic shapes. Deleting two segments that are vertically adjacent creates a door. Deleting one from the centre row creates a window. Deleting all but the bottom row creates a fence, and so on. Combining these shapes, you can create any structure you like, but in Battle Royale mode you want to keep it simple!

Use walls for quick cover

Floors

While in some modes floors can be a decorative addition to a base, you should only worry about using them for practical reasons when playing Battle Royale. Floors have a lip on the outer edge so you can easily connect a wall to them and/or create a small fence around any surface you build.

Floors are made of a 2x2 panel, so they have fewer basic shapes – only five can be rotated – and you won't want to spend long fiddling with them. In fact, most of the time you play Battle Royale mode, floors aren't much use at all – just drop a regular-shaped floor and move on.

Use floors to build towers

Stairs get you up high

140 HP

EDIT G | BUILD 10
MATERIAL | R ROTATE

127

0 | 100
100 | 100

Stairs

Stairs are more commonly called ramps – because that's what they look like – but as far as the game is concerned they're stairs! They're perfect for getting you out of a dead end or for reaching that all-important high ground. If you only learn how to build ONE thing, it should be them!

Stairs have a strange shape, which consists of four corners with eight smaller tiles between them. You can use this to create four shapes: a simple ramp (O shape), a quarter-turn (L shape), a half-turn (U shape) and a half-stair (I shape). Generally, you don't need to build more than the simple ramp, but if you have a little extra time, you may want to use the others shapes to create a better-crafted structure and save on materials usage!

Roofs

Roofs cap off the top of a building to give you defence from aerial attacks and/or items being thrown over walls. Only bother with a roof if you're planning to stay in a place long enough for people to attack you in that way. They'll stop people getting up high, and make grenades and other thrown items bounce off the side.

Roofs are made of a 2x2 grid, so they have the same basic five shapes as a floor. However, unlike floors, they're sloped when built, so this makes them a better defence. The only real advantage to building a different-shaped roof is cosmetic – if you do, try not to leave any gaps!

SMG

Editing buildings

Once you've built a structure, you can still edit it – even after construction is complete! Pressing the edit button on the controller (refer to your console or PC's instructions!) will give you access to the footprint editor, allowing you to delete certain sections. Once you confirm the edit, this will become permanent.

Be careful, though, as it's possible to edit a building so that it's no longer structurally viable, which could bring it all crashing to the ground! Editing buildings has no materials cost, so you can perform as many changes as you like, whenever you want. Just don't blame us if you get a shotgun in the back!

Edit buildings to make a door

Structures have a health bar

Roofs can be used as cover

Building health and damage

Like everything in Fortnite, buildings have a health value, which can be reduced until it's destroyed. When you place a piece of a building, it costs 10 of the relevant materials to create. The health points of the building part will then slowly increase until it reaches full strength and becomes complete. Wooden structures have the least HP and build fastest, while metal structures have the highest HP but build slower.

You can destroy an opponent's structure during the building process, and the quicker you start attacking the easier it is to destroy. Any weapon can damage both people and structures, but the damage value for structures is different – some guns cause less damage to buildings than people, and others do more.

As with any structure, you can damage player-made buildings with a pickaxe and harvest the materials they drop!

ON TARGET

Building is one half of the challenge when it comes to Fortnite – making your shots count is key to the battles themselves...

A t some point, to make progress in Fortnite, you're going to have to go on the attack! Being armed to the gills with gold weapons is no guarantee of success, though – you'll have to make sure your shots count.

Fortunately, help is at hand! For starters, take a look at the crosshairs of your weapon, since they'll give you a hefty clue as to just how accurate your shot will be. Look at how close together they are – the tighter they are, the more on target your shot is likely to be.

For maximum accuracy, stay still, crouch and zoom, if possible. The only downside of doing this is that you leave yourself very open to attack.

Factor in bullet drop

Target Practice

If you're looking to get a feel for targeting, try out the Playground Mode, where you can practise without worrying about being wiped out! Also, while you're all waiting to board the battle bus at the start of a Battle Royale, use this time to test your accuracy.

However, if you're running around, and jumping up and down, the crosshairs will move further apart and, as you might expect, your shot will end up being a lot less accurate!

As for the crosshairs themselves, they're just a guide. Your shot will land somewhere in the crosshairs, but there's no guarantee as to where. That's why it's better to get them closer together!

Shotguns can be an interesting choice: their ammo is made up of lots of little pellets, so even a poor shot can inflict a bit of damage.

Practise in the Playground Mode

Ctrl To Release A Balloon

Targeting

When it comes to aiming, you need to factor in how experienced you are. You can do the most damage with a headshot, but these are really difficult to pull off, especially when you're in a fast-moving, close-combat situation. A better idea is to aim for your opponent's upper body. It's a bigger target to hit and will still do a fair amount of damage.

Try to deal a knockout shot, unless you're fighting someone who's already taken a fair amount of damage. It's worth being ready with a follow-up shot just in case, although a second shot tends to be less accurate than the first.

If you're sniping from height, make sure you factor in some degree of bullet drop. When you're firing from a long distance, the bullet is subject to gravity. So when you fire at someone's head, you may find your shot is lucky to hit their feet! As such, aim a little above your target. If you're at a greater height, bullet drop is likely to be less of a factor.

Battle Royale is the most popular way to play Fortnite. But what is it, and what do you need to know?

FORTNITE

SEASON 5

 LEVEL 1

0 / 100 ⭐ 2

LVL 5 ⭐ 5

 BATTLE PASS
ess to weekly challenges, 🔒

FREE PASS
TIER 1   ⭐ 0 / 10

EVENT CHALLENGES

Play matches of The Getaway

0 / 10 XP 5,000

DAILY CHALLENGES

ests

0 / 7 XP 500 ⭐ 5

HOW TO PLAY

In Battle Royale, 100 players are dropped onto a map and given a simple task: to be the last one standing and earn the Victory Royale! You battle to collect weapons, ammo and resources while avoiding being caught in the constantly shrinking storm eye. Most games last 10-15 minutes, depending on how long you survive! It's also possible to play in pairs and squads.

What makes Battle Royale so exciting are its seasons. Every few weeks, a new story unfolds, changing the locations on the map and the behaviour of the game, teasing out fresh narrative and providing players with all-new entertainment!

It's one vs 100...
Good luck!

BATTLE ROYALE GUIDE

❤ 100 | 10
+ 100 | 10

IT'S BACK!

BEEF BOSS IS BACK

Not Ready

Weapon colour (in the inventory) indicates rarity

BATTLE ROYALE STRATEGY

A game of Battle Royale can be divided into beginning, middle and end, all of which require their own strategies. Here are some things you can do to smooth out your performance in each.

WEAPONS

When you start a game, you have only a pickaxe, which you can use to collect resources, but before long you'll find some weapons. There aren't many melee weapons in Battle Royale mode, but there are lots of different guns, each with their own strengths and weaknesses. Weapons are tweaked, added or removed each season, so don't rely on one too heavily!

The important thing to note about weapons is that they don't have a crafting system like in Save The World, but they DO have a rarity level that determines how good they are. White is the most common, followed by green, blue and purple. If you see an orange one, grab it immediately – it's the best!

Beginning

The lobby is a test area, so use it to familiarise yourself with weapons – you can't be hurt. When the game switches to the battle bus launch, press jump once to skydive, and a second time to deploy your glider. Don't use the glider until as late as possible, as it will slow you down!

When you land, quickly start collecting resources and weapons, and get away from any nearby players in case they find a gun before you do. At this point, the game is in the scavenging phase. Try not to get into fights, and fill up your resources and inventory.

Load up on items early

Middle

Once the storm starts shrinking, you can concentrate on a fight. You'll encounter players more frequently, so get somewhere safe and try to pick them off from a distance. You should try to head towards the centre of the safe area, so you don't get swallowed when the storm next shrinks!

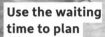

Use the waiting time to plan

End-game

This is where you have to start chasing down other players. Deploy as many weapons as you've got, and actively go after anyone who looks weak or injured. The storm will have reached its final size, so you don't have to worry about being caught. But with so little space to fight in and only the best players left, it's going to get deadly!

The end-game gets intense!

BATTLE ROYALE HINTS & TIPS

Plenty of resources to collect here

Plan your jump

When most players are running around the lobby firing ineffectually at other waiting players, the best of the best study the map so they can decide where and when to jump out of the battle bus. Check out the route the bus will take (indicated across the map by blue arrows), then stick down a map marker at the perfect place. Not too popular, not too remote.

Execute your dive

Once you're out of the bus, every second counts. You need to reach the ground as quickly as possible, so push forward to go into a downward dive, then nudge yourself slowly towards your target. You don't want to get exactly over your target – aim for a point about a grid square away from it, so when your glider deploys you can move towards it. If you're too close, you'll overshoot!

Practise building!

The best players can build huge towers in seconds by mashing the build buttons, so you need to learn to do that too. Rebinding your keys is a great way to do that, but that's just the start. It's best to pick a remote spot, then harvest enough wood so you can build in peace until the storm closes in.

Use ramps as cover

If you encounter an enemy while running across an open space, perhaps because they've just emerged from around a corner, a quickly deployed ramp will give you the cover you need to regroup. Likewise, if you find yourself being sniped at from a distance, throwing up a lot of ramps quickly will make it hard for them to continue their attack. Try to be unpredictable – lay them in different directions, run around them instead of over them – anything you can do to outfox the person who's going to EXPECT you to run straight up and over!

Don't forget resources

You have almost no resources to begin with, so if you don't stock up you're never going to build much of anything. It takes seconds to chop down a tree, so unless you're in the middle of a fight you've always got time to stock up. The worst thing that can happen mid-fight is that you discover your fort has completely emptied you of materials to use, so keep an eye on what you've got, and don't build yourself into a dead end.

Don't build off someone else's structure

If you build your base off someone else's, you're opening yourself up for a swift death. They could easily edit or destroy their part of the building to break yours, and even if they've abandoned it you leave yourself with fewer editing options! Bases aren't worth a lot in Battle Royale – the game moves so fast anyway that it's better to stay alive than worry too much about what you've built.

25

HUNTING FOR CHESTS!

To turn a Battle Royale in your favour, search for chests and get your hands on some fantastic weapons and goodies!

STORM EYE SHRINKING 6 Minutes 58 Seconds

LANDING!

When you leap off the battle bus and are coming into land, you should get a decent view of the landscape and be able to spot any chests out in the open. It's really only safe to go for these early in the game, before everyone's had chance to get hold of a weapon!

Look out for chests as you land

LISTEN!

A key way to discover a chest is by hearing it first! Get used to the sound of chests and how they get louder the closer you are. This can be really useful when you're in a building and there's perhaps a chest hidden behind a wall.

IN BUILDINGS

If you're in a house, chests tend to be hidden in the roof or the basement. The game likes to make you work, rather than making everything too obvious, so you may need to hack through walls, floors or ceilings! Roofs, in particular, can be a challenge: in bigger houses, it's not always clear which bit of the roof the chest is hiding under. Look on top of the garage attached to a house, for instance, as it may be hidden under the roof there!

There are dozens of chests just waiting to be found!

FAMILIAR PLACES

Whilst chests do change location from game to game, there are some places you can generally rely on to have one every time you play. For instance, on the very highest mountain tops, there's usually some reward for scaling such heights.

TRUCKS!

If you see a lorry parked with the back of its cargo hold open, it's worth having a look inside for chests. Just beware that you're an easy target if another player is nearby! Also look out for dumper trucks, as there tends to be a chest in the trailers of some of them. You may need to build to get to them, though – and every time you build, someone's knows you were there!

SEARCHING

As a rule of thumb, the harder a place is to access and find, the more likely it is to hold a reward. The good news is that every Battle Royale has dozens of chests just waiting to be discovered, so there's a good chance you'll get your hands on one!

Listen out for the sound of chests!

BEWARE!

Be careful using explosives around chests, as you could end up blowing them to smithereens, along with the valuable loot inside!

27

1

PART 2

101 AMAZING THINGS TO DO IN FORTNITE

So you've tackled the first set of challenges. Now here's the second set to work your way towards doing 101 awesome things in Fortnite!

Who will get there first?!

Space To Deploy Glider

35 Pick a landing target with your friends/squad members and see which of you can be the FIRST to reach it once you've exited the battle bus!

36 Make a rule that if you see an air drop, you HAVE to run for it, even if you don't want to risk getting into a fight!

37 Climb a tree then stay there for as long as possible – either until you're killed or the storm forces you to go and find another one!

38 Play the game without building at all – no walls, no ramps, nothing!

39
Match your movements to the storm. If the storm isn't moving, neither can you!

No building allowed!

40
Land near an area with a football (e.g. the stadium), then try to kick it along with you wherever you go!

41
Play the game like a ninja: you can only stop running when you make it to cover – no stopping out in the open!

42
Aside from the very first weapon you collect, you can only swap weapons when you take them from a player you've killed.

43
When you see an enemy, you must start dancing immediately until they begin to shoot at you.

44
When building, you CAN'T use stairs/ramps. If you want to climb, you'll have to do it another way!

45
Here's a fun and frustrating way to play: you aren't allowed to jump except by using jump pads. Hands off that button!

Stay in your ATK!

46
Try to play a game without fighting anyone – always run and see how long you can survive!

47
Don't stop moving the ENTIRE game, even for a second. The challenge is to keep running whenever you're able to!

48
Avoid all named areas for the entire game. You can only visit locations that aren't marked as points of interest.

49
Find an ATK, get in it and, from now on, you can't exit the vehicle at all – only driving fatalities allowed!

Jumping is not permitted!

50 For this challenge, stealth is the name of the game: you can only collect and use silenced weaponry. That means no explosives!

51 When playing in a squad, make a rule that you HAVE to all be on the same minimap at all times. No wandering off on your own!

52 When in squads, you designate one person the leader and only THEY can shoot their weapons. Everyone else is just there to carry the gear and draw fire.

53 Time to be an aerial master: you can only fire your weapon while your feet are off the ground. That means only when jumping or falling!

54 Every time you kill someone, build a 1x1 wall on the spot where they fall as a small gravestone in their honour.

55 When you kill an enemy, have your whole squad gather round and do the same emote.

56 Play with a friend (or several!) and each pick a house to demolish. First person to level theirs completely wins the challenge!

57 When starting Battle Royale, you have to be the last person off the battle bus. You can only jump

Demolish a house!

Play with no teammates

hur bludgeoned Kaizen Sushi
Ne shotgunned Marshmallowv
9 shotgunned emre_basan

when everyone else is gone!

58 Play in lonely mode: enter a squad game but choose no-fill and no teammates. Land in Lonely Lodge for extra loneliness points!

59 Become a cat burglar: if you want to enter a house, you can do it only by breaking into the roof.

60 Think you're a good shot? Play with a sniper rifle, but don't aim using the sights or a scope!

61 How about you give up the element of surprise on purpose? If you see an enemy, fire your weapon at them but DON'T hit them until they start firing at you!

62 Rather than trying to track down enemies, make them come to you – build the biggest, tallest fort you can and try to hold them off until either the storm gets you or an enemy does.

63 Play chicken. If you see an enemy, run towards them, but don't fire until they do!

Build the biggest fort

64 When the battle bus drop happens, pick a player, then spend the rest of the game trying to stay as close as possible to them WITHOUT killing them!

65 See how good you are when you don't have your stats: turn off the HUD and play that way!

66 Only use the most basic weapons: common guns only! If you pick up anything better, you have to throw it away immediately.

67 Become the sheriff of battle island: you can only attack other players if you see them attack someone else first!

68 Play follow the leader: join a squad, pick a leader, then everyone has to follow them around the map in a single-file line!

Stay close to another player

HEALTH & SHIELDS!

Here are some handy hints to help you manage your health and stay alive!

You don't need us to tell you that other Fortnite players won't think twice about taking you down. That's where keeping on top of your health comes in very handy!

Appreciating that different game modes may change the mechanics a little (some limit your health options a lot!), it's always best to keep either a shield potion or some kind of health kit in your inventory. We like slurp juice, as that replenishes both your shields AND your health.

Get your shields up to 100

55 | 100
100 | 100

16 | 0

100

Keep your shields topped up!

Obviously, the first thing you should focus on when you land on the island is making sure you get hold of a weapon of some description, but you also need to get your shields up to 100. We recommend keeping a stock of small shield potions. They may only replenish your shields to a level of 50, but they can be knocked back really quickly, which is an advantage, as speed is often of the essence in Fortnite!

This is the downside of the gold chug jugs you can find. They replenish your health and shields to 100, but they take so long to drink that you're vulnerable to attack just by downing one (and the time you generally need a chug jug is later in a battle when the storm has closed in and it's harder to find somewhere to hide!).

Even medical kits can take a while to work. Slurp Juice, however, is great as it's quick to consume – the only downside is that it doesn't replenish your shields/health instantly and takes a bit of time to kick in. Still, you can be running around causing mayhem while it patches you up!

DOING DAMAGE

When it comes to finding out if an opponent has much in the way of shields, just look at the colour of the damage number that comes up when you hit them. If it's blue, the damage has been done to their shields and their health is intact. If it's white, they don't have any shields left and you've damaged their health. A gold number means you've hit the vehicle they're travelling in and their health hasn't been affected at all!

Stock up on shield potions

28 Packets/s   4.92 KB/s
0% Packet Loss   54 Packets/s

brumgrunt

Height is a huge advantage!

Ping: 27
↑ 7.61 KB/s   ↓ 0% Packet Loss
0% Packet Loss   42 Packets/s

Improve your game to get closer to the final battle and the sweet taste of victory!

Whilst it's fun to play duo and squad games, perhaps the toughest mode to succeed in is the solo game. After all, it's you against 99 other players in a fight to the death!

So what are the tricks to getting ahead in solo? Well, it depends on what kind of player you are. If you're inexperienced, you're going to need a big slice of luck to win a match. And even if you know the game inside out, you'll need a few tricks up your sleeve to pull off a victory!

SUCCEEDING IN SOLO!

25 | 100
100 | 100

0 | 100

Traps are easy to place

THE BASICS

>> In your inventory, make sure you have some form of health or shield replenishment, ideally one weapon you can use close up, and one from a distance/an explosive. Keep your guns reloaded, and practise switching between them quickly!

>> Use cover! If you're out in the open, you're a target. Hide under trees and use the cover of buildings. If you find a secluded spot out in the open, by all means hide and lie in wait for an opponent. It's a strategy that can quickly backfire, though!

>> If you're not moving, you're easier to hit! If you're hiding, then fair enough. But standing around in the open, perhaps trying to line up a good sniping shot, leaves you vulnerable. Jump around! Move! Make yourself as hard a target as possible!

>> If you're taking advantage of planes, ground vehicles or mounted turrets, factor in that people will hear you coming. A sharpshooter can quickly end your game.

>> Some players don't like the building side of Fortnite, but it's crucial to success. At the very least, practise throwing up some quick fences in a hurry. They can buy you a few precious seconds, which may just be crucial in a shoot-out.

>> Watch the storm! It's so obvious, but in every Battle Royale game there's always a couple of people who lose track of the clock, of where the storm is, and of their way out!

>> Gather resources! If you've got 100 wood in your inventory, you know you can quickly build a ramp or two, which may just get you where you need to be a little faster!

>> Listen! It's worth playing with a decent set of headphones on, as sound is a massive giveaway that trouble is coming. If you can pick up the noise of quiet footsteps or a gun reloading from afar, you can be prepared for an incoming attack. The reverse is true, of course. Other people will be listening just as intently for you to reveal your position!

BUILDING

>> It's worth spending time in the Playground and Creative modes to practise throwing up some basic structures quickly. Ideally, you need to be able to build some quick defences and tower structures that allow you cover whilst giving you a vantage point. You're highly unlikely to win a Battle Royale match without building something!

>> Consider your materials. A wooden fence is great for a quick bit of protection, but if you're building yourself a sniper nest, for instance, a brick structure is a better bet. Always be on the lookout for the resources you need too!

>> If you keep stumbling when needing to throw up a ramp in a hurry, try reassigning your controls to something that suits you a little more.

Find chests, and fast!

Master close combat

55 eliminated gameur4749 with a trap

E Swap

Head for the hills!

Turret guns are good, but you're an easy target!

ATTACKING TIPS

>> Height is a huge advantage! Not only are you harder to hit, but you also have a better chance of landing a clear shot on a target. Tops of trees aren't bad spots for snipers, but if you're a sharpshooter and you can get a high-up vantage point, you're in a very strong position.

>> When sniping a long distance, you need to factor in that your bullet will drop a little when flying through the air. As such, aim above your target, and practise doing so to factor this in.

>> The bit where everybody's preparing to go on the battle bus at the start of a match? Use that time to practise close-up shooting. Find a target, and jump around them – making yourself harder to hit in the process – and get used to landing shots when you're on the move.

DEFENDING TIPS

>> Sometimes the safer thing to do is to get up and run away. Not always easy, of course, but if a firefight is looking hopeless, and you perhaps have a portal through which you can make a quick escape, take the coward's way out and live to fight another day!

>> The most effective defence involves throwing up a building or defensive structure, and keeping moving. Letting off three balloons at once and zooming into the sky helps too!

Plan your landing!

AND ALSO

When a balloon is dropping and you want to keep the loot to yourself, build a wall around where it's going to land. That makes it harder for others to muscle in! Do note that it will attract unwanted attention, though...

Whether you've played Fortnite or not, chances are you've come across flossing! But where did it come from, and can you do it in real life?!

FLOSS
LIKE A
BOSS!

Amongst the many emotes you can pick up in Fortnite (at the time of going to print at least) is the floss, which is by far the most popular! Its origins lie with a performer by the name of Backpack Kid (real name Russell Horning), who first performed the dance on American TV back in 2017. Little did he know what a huge phenomenon he was set to inspire!

Fortnite introduced the floss emote way back in Season 2. It soon became a very firm favourite, and its popularity has even spilled over into the real world too!

If you haven't yet worked out how to dance in Fortnite, it's simple! If you're using a game controller, just press down on the D pad, and if you're playing on a computer, press the B key.

You'll have access to only a few dance emotes initially, but Fortnite gives them out as rewards as you progress through the game, or you can buy more with V-Bucks – but that costs you money!

Epic continues to add more and more emotes to the game. Whilst flossing is the highest profile, it's far from the only dance in town. Still, after you've taken out a particularly taxing opponent, who wouldn't want a quick boogie to celebrate?!

HOW TO FLOSS!

You don't have to look far on YouTube for videos showing you how to floss in real life. But if you want a quick checklist, here's what you need to know:

☐ **Face the front.** Move your shoulders a little forward. Move your feet slightly apart. With your hands, make fists.

☐ **Keep both of your arms straight**, and swing them to the left. At the same time, move your hips to the right.

☐ **Next, your arms have to come back to your body**, then to the right, all in one go! Make sure you keep your arms straight while you do it. One arm needs to be in front of the other, and as your arms go right, move your hips left!

☐ **Then you need to do the above step in reverse**! Arms to the left, hips to the right!

☐ **Repeat!** And gradually get faster as you find your rhythm. In no time, you'll be flossing like a boss!

WEBSITES

Fortnite News

Do you want to discover some secrets about your favourite game? Then get yourself over to this unofficial source of Fortnite news and see what the developers have in store for you. The site is jam-packed with leaked information about forthcoming items, game modes and cosmetics. There are also lots of details about the latest patches and the goodies they contain. It's a great way to stay ahead of the game, and your friends are sure to become envious of your in-depth knowledge!

tinyurl.com/FortniteAnnual1

@FortniteGame

Even if you're too young to have a Twitter account, you can still read Fortnite's official tweets without signing up. Here you can check out new outfits in the Item Shop, keep up to date with any tech issues affecting the game, and see short videos of the coolest new things you can do. The feed is updated many times a day, so why not take a look before you launch into each gaming session?

tinyurl.com/FortniteAnnual2

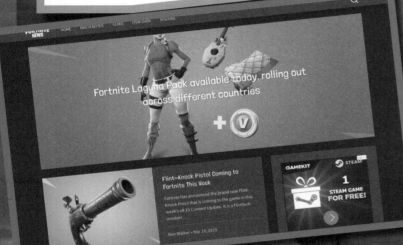

WEBSITES AND YOUTUBERS

Want to get the best out of Fortnite? Here are some top YouTubers and websites!

Fortnite Insider

Fortnite Insider doesn't seem to be dishing out many new tips these days, but there are still plenty of them to get your teeth into. They're mixed in with lots of news and information about the game, as well as a section of leaked skins. Best of all, there's a link to a 3D Fortnite Cosmetic creator that lets you select an outfit, back bling, pickaxe and background. See what combo you can come up with!

tinyurl.com/FortniteAnnual3

Fortnite Tracker

With more stats than you can shake a pickaxe at, Fortnite Tracker lets you enter your Epic name to discover how well you're doing. You get to view your win total, win percentage and the number of kills you've achieved. There are also separate stats for solo, duo and squad plays, as well as a rundown of your recent matches. Once you've revelled in your glory, check out the leaderboards and then take a look at the latest trends.

tinyurl.com/FortniteAnnual4

Official Fortnite Website

Reckon you were done with the official Fortnite site after downloading the game? Maybe it's time to have another look. Click Watch, and you can sit back and chill while viewing some stunning moves by other players. Head over to Competitive, and you can keep an eye on in-game competitions that have rewards and prizes for top performers. There's even a load of merch that you may want to add to your present lists.

tinyurl.com/FortniteAnnual5

Account Merge

Yeah, it's boring admin stuff, but if you have two console logins that you want to bring together, this is where you need to do it. Just enter a primary account from Xbox One, Switch or PS4 and then choose a secondary account to merge it with. It will take a fortnight for your Fortnite Cosmetic Items and V-Bucks to transfer!

tinyurl.com/FortniteAnnual6

Font Generator

If you love the Fortnite font and you want to write something in the same style (your name perhaps?), then launch this website and tap away at the keyboard. Alter the font size, choose a colour and create a PNG image of your words when you're done.

tinyurl.com/FortniteAnnual7

Ninja

Ninja is a professional Battle Royale Player and he's proud to have bagged first place in the Fortnite Celebrity Pro-Am Tournament at E3 in 2018. It means you can expect a good dose of serious skills to ooze from the screen in his videos, and he often does so while attempting some rather good impressions. We love how he not only shows himself but his hands as he moves the mouse and the keys with the greatest of subtlety but with devastating effect.

tinyurl.com/FortniteAnnual9

YOUTUBERS

Nick Eh 30

Cheery chappie Nick Eh 30 posts a new video every Sunday, and his enthusiasm for Fortnite is infectious. Not only does he showcase some neat moves (with a look of intense concentration on his face), his funny moments compilations are hilarious. Each video is worth the watch, and they're almost (stress, almost) as good as playing the game yourself.

tinyurl.com/FortniteAnnual8

Typical Gamer

With more than eight million subscribers, Typical Gamer is certainly popular. He's also a decent guy: even when he made a kid cry in one of his videos, they were tears of joy – the player was just chuffed at being able to chat and play with his hero! Typical Gamer's enthusiasm for Fortnite is clear, and he'll cheerily engage with other players, often accompanying his play with a chuckle and a song.

tinyurl.com/ FortniteAnnual10

ONE_shot_GURL

Julie's live streams are full of enthusiasm, and she clearly loves getting stuck into Fortnite and having a real blast. She once teamed up with Nick Eh 30, FaZe Cloak and Tfue to ratchet up an impressive 53 squad kills, so tune in each day for her skilful gaming displays. Julie's interactions with other players are definite highlights, and her easy-going manner makes her Fortnite's true gaming queen.

tinyurl.com/FortniteAnnual11

Fortnite

Need to up your game? With Fortnite's official YouTube channel, you can learn how to create lots of cool things in the game's Creative mode. It pulls player-made videos into a dedicated, curated playlist. The channel also showcases lots of great moves and features so you get a good flavour of what to expect yourself. Head over to the Community sections and there are some wonderful dev updates. These guys obviously know their game well, so be sure to keep tuning in.

tinyurl.com/FortniteAnnual12

The Story of Fortnite Episode 1

Top5Gaming

For anyone who loves history, Top5Gaming has a great lesson for you. It takes a look at how Fortnite came to be, starting by exploring Seasons 1 and 2 when there were no skins or battle passes to be seen. Each episode lasts for around 10 to 13 minutes, so they won't severely eat into your playing time. There are also lots of other great videos, including seasons that are ranked from worst to best and the biggest noob skins you should never wear.

tinyurl.com/FortniteAnnual13

Fortnite 247

Like to watch fails? Fortnite 247 is full of quirky, funny moments from across the globe. From people accidentally eliminating themselves to wireless controllers giving up at the worst possible moment, there's much to chuckle at in these compilations. They just keep coming too, so even if you have some bad moments, you can rest knowing that others have probably had worse.

tinyurl.com/FortniteAnnual14

43

PART 3

101 AMAZING THINGS TO DO IN FORTNITE

Congratulations! You've made it to the final set of 101 things to do in our favourite game. Complete these to become a true Fortnite pro!

Play with a friend

🛡 **Cyphr Wond3r** ⊙ 1

69 Do some base jumping! When you leave the battle bus, aim for the roof of a building. If you don't land on it, you have to stay exactly where you are for the rest of the game.

70 Play in a duo with a friend. One of you only collects ammo, the other only collects weapons!

71 Use the scope on a sniper rifle permanently. No coming out of scope mode!

72 See if you and your squad can destroy a building using only rockets fired from a distance.

Stay off the grass!

73 Create a large, high ramp and hide near the base. When another player runs up, jump out and delete the bottom piece to send the whole thing plummeting!

74 Keep off the grass – you can only travel on highways and pavements. No shortcuts over open ground!

75 Find the bunker and guard the entrance. Don't let ANYONE in.

76 When you've drunk a shield potion, don't fire your weapons. Just walk slowly and directly towards your enemy, and see if you can spook them!

77 Find a cabin in the woods and stay there as long as you can. Set up a campfire and let other players join you if they don't attack!

78 Only heal yourself using mushrooms for an entire game.

79 Land on one edge of the map and try to cross to the other side before the storm eye shrinks too much, then see if you can get back too!

Have a smashing time!

Set up a campfire in a cabin

80 Make yourself a piñata-smashing challenge. See how many you can find and break in one round, then try to beat that record in the next game!

81 Plough ALL of the resources you collect into vending machines, even if you don't need what they're offering.

82 Race a friend (or several!) around the racetrack. No guns, obviously, but crashing into each other is fair game!

83 Try to kill an opponent just by destroying their fort rather than shooting weapons or explosives at them.

84 Don't shoot ANYONE and see how long you can survive. Keep a note of your best position so that you can try to break the record.

85 Write out the numbers 1 to 100 in a list, then cross them off as you finish in that place. See how long it takes to finish in EVERY position.

86 Collect several jump pads and see how many you can bounce on in a row – you'll have to place them JUUUUST right!

87 Choose a small-ish location such as Junk Junction and spend the entire round trying to raze it flat!

88 Find the drive-thru at Risky Reels and, if there are enough cars (it changes all the time!), see if you can harvest them ALL for materials.

89 Choose a high mountain peak and see which of your friends can reach the top first.

90 Play a game of tag across the entire map – if you take damage from a friend's melee weapon that means you're tagged and become "it".

91 Hold a dance party! Pick a location such as the disco warehouses and dance the round away there. Even

Raze it flat!

Finish in every position!

Get chopping!

if you're attacked, keep on dancing!

92 Find two buildings and see whether you can jump from one to the other without falling. It will be just like *The Matrix!*

93 Forget ATKs – from now on the only transportation you can use is a shopping cart! If you're not in a shopping cart, you HAVE to crouch so that you walk slowly.

94 If you're playing in a squad, separate to the four corners of the map when the round starts and stay apart until there are just 10 players left in the game.

95 Spend the entire game running backwards. It's harder than it sounds and you'll definitely end up doing something hilarious!

96 Make a treehouse by building a wooden base on top of a tree once you've climbed up it.

97 Find a vending machine, then build your own shop around it out of metal. Let people "buy" items from you as long as they don't attack!

98 Become a lumberjack! Destroy as many trees as possible. Try to convince other people to help you!

99 You can only kill people using C4. Try to lure them towards your explosives by making them chase you!

100 Treat your bullets with respect: reload every time you fire a shot.

101 Become a hoarder and collect every item you find. You have to ALWAYS collect it, even if that means dropping something good!

Build a shop around a vending machine

Deposit Wood (300)

EXPERT TIPS

Want to play like a pro in Battle Royale mode? Well, here are our top tips, tricks and shortcuts to help you do just that!

Land in unpopulated areas

You've probably heard this advice tonnes of times throughout this book, but it is the #1 way to stay alive if you're not a sharpshooter. When you jump out of the battle bus, you'll see others falling at the same time as you – your goal is to stay AWAY from them!

Sound effects will give away your position

Stay low during a fight

When you do get into a gunfight, don't start running around as it makes it impossible for you to line up your shots. Get behind some cover, crouch down and use the camera to observe the other player. Hang back, stayed crouched and only THEN pop bullets at them from a distance. You'll be more accurate and harder to see/hit.

Keep your ears open

Always listen out for sound effects – especially gunfire – which may indicate that other players are nearby. If you hear some close to you, stop moving and try to figure out where it's coming from so you can prepare to shoot.

Be a team player!

In Duo and Squad modes, make sure you know where your team is planning to land so that you can assist one another as soon as you hit the ground. When playing in a team, remember not to hoard everything for yourself! Always revive your teammates if you can, and share items so that no one is left without a decent with which weapon to engage the enemy!

Know the best place to get materials

This is easy to keep track of, but just so you're not confused, trees/palettes are the best source of wood, because they break quickly. Giant rocks are the best source of stone. And cars/vehicles are the best source of metal.

Keep low to stay safe

Control your fire rate

Just because your gun eats bullets, that doesn't mean it HAS to. Even if your weapon is fully automatic, shoot in small bursts to maintain accuracy. If you hold down fire, the bullets will spread out a lot!

Try to cause fall damage

A three-storey drop is enough to kill a player, so if you see someone building up high, don't shoot at them – try to shoot the floor beneath them! They might not even know what's happening until it's too late.

Jump further with a pulse grenade

Whether you need a quick exit from a fight or you just want to gain the upper hand on your opponent, getting a boost from your own pulse grenade is an essential move for the advanced player. They can propel you huge distances, and the blast itself doesn't cause any damage. Try to ride the edge of the blast so that you're thrown horizontally, not upwards!

Make sure the cover is on your left

While some games give you the ability to switch the hand your gun is in, Fortnite only gives you one option. This means if you're hiding behind some cover to your right, you can't easily pop out to shoot without exposing your entire body to harm. Always keep the cover on your left.

Pulse grenades can give you a boost

F1   F2   F3   49 F4

THE BIG FORTNITE QUIZ

Reckon you're a Fortnite expert? Take our big quiz and put your knowledge to the test!

In what year was Fortnite first officially made available?

A   2016
B   2017
C   2018

2 Which of these was NOT a location in Battle Royale Season 1?

A   Anarchy Acres
B   Moisty Mine
C   Tilted Towers

3 What is the name of Fortnite's in-game currency?

A   V-Bucks
B   V-Dollars
C   V-Coins

4 A meteor hit the Fortnite island and created Dusty Divot at the start of which season?

A   Season 3
B   Season 4
C   Season 5

5 What were the rocks that, when your picked them up, allowed you to jump much higher?

A   Hop rocks
B   Jump rocks
C   Leap rocks

6 How many shield points does one small shield potion give you?

A   25
B   50
C   75

9 Which of these is an epic rarity emote?

A   Dab
B   Face Palm
C   Drop The Bass

10 What colour are rare weapons in the game?

A   Blue
B   Purple
C   Green

8 In what season was the Battle Pass introduced in Fortnite?

A   Season 1
B   Season 2
C   Season 3

7 Which movie villain has been known to make an appearance in Fortnite?

A   The T-1000
B   Thanos
C   Venom

11 If you want your opponent to stop what they're doing and dance, what do you need to throw at them?

A   Dance Bomb
B   Jump Bomb
C   Boogie Bomb

13 Which of these used to be in the bottom right of the Fortnite map?

A   Prison
B   Football stadium
C   Golf course

12 In squares, how big is the Fortnite Battle Royale?

A   8 x 8
B   9 x 9
C   10 x 10

14 What destroyed Wailing Woods?

A   Iceberg
B   Volcano
C   Rocket strike

15 Which of these DOESN'T give you health points?

A   Bandage
B   Apple
C   Mushroom

16 Which of these vehicles appeared in Fortnite Battle Royale first?

A   Golf cart
B   Plane
C   Shopping trolley

19 Which of these is NOT a resource to build with in the game?

A   Metal
B   Stone
C   Concrete

20 Which of these can you build via a hotkey?

A   Pyramid
B   Ramp
C   Stairs

18 Which company makes Fortnite?

A   Easy Games
B   Epic Games
C   Amazing Games

HOW DID YOU DO?

18-20 You're a Fortnite master! Well done!

13-17 Top performance! You're in the top 25 of a Battle Royale!

8-12 You were doing well, but got sniped when you weren't looking!

4-7 A brave performance, but still room for improvement

0-3 A good try, but you need a bit more practice! Keep going!

17 Which of these explosive items does the most damage?

A   Dynamite
B   Clinger
C   Stink bomb

ANSWERS

1 B
2 C
3 B
4 A
5 B
6 B
7 A
8 A
9 C
10 A
11 C
12 C
13 A
14 C
15 C
16 B
17 B
18 B
19 B
20 B